10-MINUTE

Decorating IDEAS

KariAnne Wood

TEN PEAKS PRESS®
EUGENE, OR

Contents

Introduction ◆ 4

Spring ◆ 7

Summer ◆ 45

Fall ◆ 83

Winter ◆ 121

Introduction

Raise your hand if the thought of decorating your coffee table overwhelms you.

Raise your hand if arranging books on your bookshelf makes you want to run for the hills.

Raise your hand if you have decorating hopes and dreams and plans and ideas, but you don't know where to start.

Oh, sweet friend. Please come sit by me.

I know this looks like a decorating book. But truly? It's so much more. It's a book about taking the overwhelming out of decorating, finding joy in the everyday, and celebrating those tiny little decorating victories that show up when we least expect them. This book and its tips are all about making small changes to your spaces that add up to a home that's uniquely, wonderfully, completely you.

And the best part? All you need to get started is ten minutes.

I know, *right*? That's it.

Ten tiny, wonderful, amazing, incredible minutes.

I'm going to tell you a secret that so many people don't understand about decorating. It doesn't have to be hard. It doesn't have to be complicated. Successful decorating is truly about making small, consistent, clever changes over time to transform your house into a home.

And that's why I wrote *10-Minute Decorating Ideas*.

You see, this book is full of ideas, inspiration, arrangements, simple

DIYs, and creative ways of looking at things that you already have in your home. And the best part? It's designed to be used all year. There are sections of the book devoted to spring, summer, fall, and winter. Each group of seasonal tips and ideas shows you how to add beauty, warmth, and celebration to your home throughout all 365 days of the year.

You see, each season is special and unique and has its own scents and sights and decor perspective.

Spring is all about decorating with nests and vintage cutting boards and creating paper pots and making spring branches look like a piece of sculpture from the Metropolitan Museum of Art.

Summer is spent turning pineapples into vases and decorating with baskets and turning shells into tic-tac-toe games and creatively displaying wood beads that would win you a blue ribbon at the county fair.

Fall shows up with dough bowls full of pumpkins, pine-cone displays and paper-bag leaf garlands, and table runners that make pillows look so cozy you'll want to offer them hot chocolate.

Winter brings bottle-brush tree displays and scented pine cones, pom-pom Christmas tree pillows and wood-slice branches and surfaces decorated with all the winter wonderland the season can bring.

These pages are full of all the ideas.

All the projects. All the joy just waiting to be discovered.

My wonderful, incredible, amazing friend—all of this is yours for the taking.

Won't you join me? Let's decorate together.

I've got ten minutes. How about you?

Spring

Some people know it's spring when the flowers start to bloom and tiny blades of grass pop up across the lawn. Me? It's never truly the new season around here until I see my first sign of spring—literally.

A multi-family yard sale sign.

Here are 18 ideas and projects to get your home ready for spring.

Spring Planter
Dough Bowl

Have you shopped your house or attic yet? Did you check in aisle seven for a dough bowl? A dough bowl is one of the easiest ways to make a statement on your dining table or coffee table. To recreate this spring centerpiece look, purchase small flowerpots from your local grocery or home-improvement store. You can either select flowers that are all the same color for a unified display, or alternate colors in the arrangement.

Then place the flowerpots in the bottom of the wood dough bowl. Choose flowers with larger leaves and blooms to fill up the entire dough bowl with spring blooms. In addition, make sure each of the smaller pots have a saucer to keep the dirt from spilling over onto the bottom of the dough bowl when you water the flowers.

EXPERT TIP

Make sure to add pots in odd numbers to keep the display visually interesting.

Vintage Cutting-Board

Plate Rack

Did you know that plate racks are the superheroes of the decorating world even though they don't wear capes? Why? They don't take up much space. They are easy to collect. They are great for storage, and they can fill up an empty wall in a single bound. And they aren't just for plates anymore. Here's a fun 10-minute decorating idea to completely revamp your plate rack.

Fill it up with a collection of vintage cutting boards.

Start by shopping yard sales and thrift stores for vintage cutting boards in all different shapes and sizes. Look for cutting boards with interesting features, like distressed surfaces and jute hangers. Then add your collection to your plate rack. Arrange the cutting boards both vertically and horizontally on the racks to mix up the display.

EXPERT TIP
You can also create your own cutting boards
with leftover countertop pieces or wooden trays.

Creative Basket Storage

There's an entire basket family reunion going on at my house right now. I think they all showed up a while back in RVs with potato casseroles and matching T-shirts. *Truth?* Baskets are amazing for storage and decorating and last-minute picnics. But where do you put all those extra baskets when you aren't using them?

Here's a 10-minute idea for creative basket storage.

Hang them from a coat rack tree. The pegs on a coat rack are perfect for basket handles. Simply loop the handles over the edges of the pegs and twist the baskets from side to side to create a basket storage display that is functional and pretty all at the same time. Nest smaller baskets inside larger baskets on the display to maximize storage.

EXPERT TIP

If floor space is at a premium, store baskets in a similar way on a row of peg wall hooks.

Framed Map
Wall Art

I use my GPS to tell me where to go. And my maps? Now I use them to decorate. This blue-and-white plat map from the 1900s was discovered in the drawer of a yard-sale find. It shows the original street map from when our house was built.

To recreate this project, take a map (a page from an atlas, a printout of a street map from a special place, or a historic map from your grandmother's attic) and frame it in a floating frame with glass or plastic on both sides and a clip-on frame around the edges. The floating frame showcases the edges of the map and allows distressed corners to shine. You can find floating frames in a variety of sizes, shapes, colors, and materials.

> **EXPERT TIP**
> Create a wall of art by cutting up a large map into individual sections, framing each section, and then hanging them together to recreate the large map.

Boho Basket Makeover

Every basket dreams of the day when its agent contacts it to tell it Hollywood is calling. This ten-minute basket mini-makeover turns even the plainest of baskets into a star. To recreate this project, you'll need a wood bead strand (individual wood beads would work as well), a basket, paint, sandpaper, and hot glue.

Start by lightly roughing the center of the basket with sandpaper. Then paint the basket a color that matches your décor and let the paint dry. Next, use hot glue to attach the strand of beads to the center of the basket. Let the glue dry and then decorate.

You could add even more interest to your basket by painting the basket two different colors on either side of the beads, or by adding fringe under the strand of beads, or even by adding a tassel to the top.

EXPERT TIP
Look for wood beads in different shapes or colors to take your basket project to the next level.

Blue-and-White
Pom-Pom Pillow

Just between us? I think this world would be a much better place if every pillow had a pom-pom. These blue and white pom-pom pillows are one of my all-time favorite projects. It's my take on a much higher-end pillow, and it only takes about ten minutes to put together.

You just need a pillow cover, a pencil, a strand of tassels, scissors, cardboard, fabric glue, and a pillow insert.

Start with a premade white pillow cover with a hidden zipper. With a pencil, lightly mark a diagram of where you want the pom-poms to go on the front of the pillow. I added five rows of five pom-poms, with the pom-poms spaced out evenly in each row. Next, take a strand of tassels and clip them apart.

Place a piece of cardboard between the front and back of the pillow cover. Then fluff out the ends of the tassels to look like pom-poms. Use fabric glue to attach them to the pillow cover on your pencil marks. Let the glue dry, and fill the decorated cover with a down pillow insert.

EXPERT TIP

For another pom-pom pillow project, you could also use fabric glue to add a strand of pom-poms around the outer edge of the pillow cover.

Spring Grocery-Store
Flower Arrangement

Did you know that a $5 grocery-store flower bundle doesn't have to look like it came from the checkout stand at your local market? Here's how to spend just $5 on flowers and turn them into a creative centerpiece.

The secret? Just shop your yard. Start by cutting greenery from the yard to add to the flower arrangement. Then open up the plastic sleeve of the grocery-store flowers. Separate the stems and spread them out to check for brown leaves or damaged blooms. Using clippers, trim the ends of the flower stems at an angle. Measure your flowers against the height of the vase.

Place the greenery from the yard inside the vase as a base and layer in the flowers from the grocery store. By adding the greenery, you can almost double the size of your floral arrangement without spending another dime.

EXPERT TIP
Trim the leaves from the bottom of the flower stems to make your arrangement last longer.

Dinner on the Lawn
Place Setting

I like my place settings like I like my dinners—with a little bit of extra green. What is it about spring that makes us want to bring the outdoors in? With this place setting you can have your lawn and eat on it too.

You can find small segments of artificial turf like this at most craft stores. I cut it into placemats and set them on the table with a blue-and-white runner. Then I juxtaposed a vintage cutting board with gold cutlery and layers of patterned dishes and blue-and-white mugs.

A blue-and-white napkin is folded and placed under the edge of the dishes and the place setting is topped off with fresh sprigs of rosemary from my herb garden, tied with velvet ribbon.

EXPERT TIP

Tie bundles of fresh herbs that match your menu, and encourage guests to sprinkle fresh herbs over their plated meal.

A Tisket-Tasket
Spring Front Door

Every tisket and tasket needs a basket. Just like this simple and creative ten-minute front-door decorating idea. Instead of a wreath? Why not decorate the door with all the flowers of spring? This front-door idea is as fresh as the petals in a garden bed.

To recreate this look, you'll need a basket about 15 inches tall with a handle at the top, a ribbon, and a plastic vase or cup that fits inside the basket. Fill the vase with water and arrange the flowers, making sure to vary the heights of the stems in the arrangement. Thread a ribbon through the handle at the top of the basket and tie it onto a Command hook or nail on the door. Fluff the flowers and your door is ready to celebrate spring.

EXPERT TIP
If your basket is narrow, simply use self-watering tips for the ends of the stems instead of a vase.

Hardware *Refresh*

My hardware looked like it just finished an ironman competition. But instead of replacing it, I decided to try to refresh it. And it worked. Take a tip from me—before you replace or discard your hardware because it isn't shiny enough—STOP. Here's a time-saving and money-saving ten-minute tip that will make your hardware look almost brand-new.

All you need is a product called Rub 'n Buff. It's sold at most hardware and home improvement stores, and it comes in a small tube. It comes in different metal hues, but my favorite color is Antique Gold. Follow the instructions on the tube and apply a SMALL (I cannot overemphasize the importance of that statement) amount with an applicator to the metal hardware that you want to refresh. Continue to rub until all the product is absorbed into the metal. Your hardware will be ready to use after the product sets a short while.

EXPERT TIP

If you want to keep a more vintage look and feel to your hardware, simply apply the product sparingly, allowing some of the original finish to shine through.

Nest Decorating Ideas

Nests and spring have a secret handshake, maybe because they have new life and new beginnings and fresh starts in common. But what do you do with a nest? How can you use nests to decorate? Here are four clever ideas for adding a little more nest to your spring:

- Add a nest to a wreath. This wood branch wreath is full of spring blooms and burlap and buffalo-check eggs. Simply tuck a nest into the branches to complete the look.

- Place a nest under a cloche. Somehow, a cloche makes everything cuter, and a nest is no exception.

- Tuck nests into tiny drawers. Collect nests of different sizes and shapes and place them inside a vintage piece to create a way to display your collection.

- Use them to hold down napkins. Looking for a way to keep your napkins organized? Use a nest as a napkin weight at your next party.

Layer Your *Rugs*

If you and your rugs are watching your pennies, this simple ten-minute tip will create a brand-new look for your space without breaking the budget.

Truth? Large rugs for a room can be so expensive. Instead of choosing a pricey patterned rug, find a large, inexpensive indoor/outdoor rug in a pretty neutral pattern for less than a third of the price. You may even have a large neutral rug somewhere that you overlooked because it seemed too plain for the room.

And now, layer in a much more affordable smaller rug in a pattern that works in the space. The key to making rug layering work is imperfection. Turn the two rugs at angles when you layer them to make them look purposeful.

EXPERT TIP

If you are looking to add a little more coziness to your floor, you can even layer a third smaller rug with extra texture.

Paper Spring Pot

I never met a dollar-store aisle I didn't like. There's something about the hunt for buried dollar-store treasure that makes me want to turn cartwheels. Small topiaries and potted plants like these are some of my favorite finds.

The challenge?

Most of the pots that hold these plants are simply not cute. No worries. Never let an ugly planter pot come between you and a little spring decorating. Simply cut a strip of brown craft paper (or a brown paper bag) and fold it in half to make it even sturdier. Then fold down the top of the folded paper one more time to create a rim for your paper planter, wrap it around the edges of the base of the plant and glue in place.

EXPERT TIP

If brown paper won't work with your decor, use patterned scrapbook paper that matches your room instead.

Herb Kitchen Island

About two years ago I gave up chocolate chip cookies and started making better food choices that rhyme with froccoli. To say it has been life changing is the understatement of the year. One thing I have learned along the way? To make it all work, I needed to have healthy choices at my fingertips.

Like this herb kitchen island.

To create a display like this, start with a tiered tray or stand. Next, gather a collection of your favorite herbs and place them in burlap or terra-cotta pots. Finally, place the herbs on the tiered tray in a low, flat basket in the center of the kitchen island.

Now you have an easy way to add a little flavor to your spring.

EXPERT TIP

If you want to take it to the next level, stencil the names of the herbs on the planter pots in the display.

DIY Jute Twine *Nest*

I wish I knew who created jute twine so I could send them a thank you note. Jute twine looks so utilitarian, but it's here for the heavy lifting when you're decorating. It's one of the most overlooked materials to decorate with.

Here's a simple ten-minute DIY jute twine nest. You just need twine, scissors, craft glue, small bowls, and plastic wrap.

To create a nest like this, start by cutting 18 pieces of twine that are each 12 inches long. Soak them in glue to make them pliable. Flip over a small bowl or container the size of the nest you want to create and cover it with a piece of plastic wrap. Then layer on the pieces of twine over the bowl. Let the "nest" dry in place. Once it's dry, flip it over and peel the plastic wrap off the dried pieces of twine.

Trim the edges to even out the sides of your nest.

EXPERT TIP

You can vary the size of the nests to match your display—just vary the sizes of your containers.

Plate Decorating Ideas

When you are at a decorating crossroads without an idea in your pocket? Decorate with a plate. Plates are inexpensive and versatile and collectible, and they even stack themselves for easy storage.

Here are four clever ideas for decorating with plates:

- Create a faux plate rack in your kitchen cabinets. Use tall wooden plate racks stacked end to end to mimic the look of higher-end cabinet racks. Then add the plates to the rack on the cabinet shelf.

- Hang a plate on a wall. I have used metal plate hangers, but there are a variety of different plate hanger options on the market.

- Decorate with plate storage. Layer plates and cups and dishes on the shelves of a pantry. The plates look cute, and they are there at the ready whenever you need them.

- Use patterned plates on a bookshelf in the living room. Create visual interest by lining the shelves of a bookcase with rows of plates.

Simple *Candlestick* Hack

Excess candle wax is on my list of least favorite things. It's messy. It's drippy. It's just generally too much. I tried so many different solutions with my candles, but the wax just kept melting.

And then?

I discovered these.

I replaced the candles in my candlesticks with battery-operated candles. They come in so many different shades and types and use two AA batteries. I simply removed the existing candles and cleaned out all the melted wax, and the battery-operated candles fit perfectly into my candle holders.

They have a timer that I set to come on every night, and now I use my candles on my mantel, in my windows, and on my sideboard.

All without a drop of candle wax.

EXPERT TIP
If you like the look of melting wax on candles, they sell battery operated candles with faux dripping wax that looks real without all the mess.

Shop Your *Yard* Display

You are having a party and need an instant centerpiece. The food is ready, the activities are planned, and the guests are on their way. But then you realize you forgot a table display, and you don't have much time to decorate. What's a DIY party planner to do?

Shop your yard.

Yep. It's one of the easiest and most inexpensive ways to decorate a table.

Head outside with your yard clippers and snip off a few branches of greenery. Gather a few different types of branches with leaves of different sizes. Make sure to remove the leaves below the water line to ensure the display will last.

Then place the branches in a clear glass vase filled with water. Fluff and arrange the leaves.

That's it. Instant centerpiece, just in time for the first knock on the door.

EXPERT TIP
You can also just add branches without leaves to the display for additional texture.

Summer

I live in Texas, where summer never met a triple-digit hot day it didn't like.

Summer decorating for me is all about easy. Projects that don't take much time or effort, leaving time left over for one of the best things about summer.

Sweet tea.

Here are 18 ideas and projects to get your home ready for the lazy days of summer.

Shell Tic-Tac-Toe

Have you ever discovered how hard it is to walk on the beach without picking up shells? Shells are so beautiful and come in so many different colors and patterns, and before you know it—you have an entire shell collection filling your pocket.

Then what? What happens to all those shells?

Here is a simple summer DIY that decorates and entertains all at the same time—a shell tic-tac-toe game.

All you need is a square board, some shells, and craft paint. I used a tic-tac-toe board from a game set, but you could make your own by taping off and painting lines on the board in a hashtag pattern. Then use shells as your game pieces. I used two different shapes of shells for the *X*s and *O*s.

> **EXPERT TIP**
> These would make the cutest displays at an outdoor party—guests can play at their table.

Wall Chair Display

I'm always trying to think up ways to decorate with items that also have a purpose. You know, where stacks of plates decorate shelves until they are ready to be used, blankets are stacked in baskets waiting for a cozy afternoon, and books are holding up my topiary until I need something to read.

But this ten-minute decorating idea takes the concept to the next level. Seriously.

Why not create a wall display with extra seating?

Here I added a large bicycle hook to the wall (make sure to find a stud in the wall so it's extra sturdy) and simply placed the wooden chair on the bicycle hook. The chair creates art that's actually useful.

Now it's a wall display just waiting for a party to happen.

EXPERT TIP
On a larger wall you could add a row of chairs for additional seating with this purposeful wall art.

Creative
Coffee Table Idea

In amazing decorating news—coffee tables don't always have to start out life as coffee tables. You can repurpose crates and wooden pulleys and ottomans and planters and vintage spools as coffee tables. All you need is a little coffee table imagination.

Or a vintage game table. Like this one.

A long time ago in a land far away, this table was used for chess and backgammon and cribbage.

And now it's still playing games. Just more of the furniture variety.

The size and details and game boards make it an interesting piece to repurpose as a coffee table. Use this as inspiration, and look around your spaces. What do you have at your house that you could repurpose as a table or furniture piece?

EXPERT TIP

One of the easiest ways to create a side table is to layer a stack of books. Simply turn the books at angles to give stability to the stack and place it beside a chair.

Charcuterie
Summer Place Setting

A year ago I didn't even know how to say "charcuterie."

And now? I want to create one for every gathering. Charcuterie boards are such an easy way to bring family and friends together around the table. You can fill charcuterie boards with meats and cheeses and breads and dipping sauces that are sure to make everyone's palette happy.

Here's a fresh take on charcuterie for summer.

This summer place setting starts with a round natural-fiber placemat and a cream charger. The next layer is a khaki-and-white raised plate with extra personality and a bird design. Lastly, there's a mini charcuterie board on top of the plate. You can add individual meats and cheeses and bread to the mini board on the place setting, or just set a larger board in the center of the table for guests to add their selections to their mini board.

EXPERT TIP
You also can personalize each charcuterie board for your guests with their name or monogram.

Summer *Shell* Vase

If you know, you know. The best way to make a flower arrangement fancy is to start with a glass vase and add something to use as a base for the flowers. I've seen lemons and limes, glass beads, cork, and driftwood all used as vase fillers.

But in the summer?

What is a better way to fill a glass vase than with shells?

Start with a clear glass vase and select shells of varying sizes and colors and fill the bottom of the vase with the shells. Then add water and arrange the flowers in the vase. The shells elevate the vase full of flowers and add a little summer to the display. The shells also act like a floral frog and help to hold the flowers in place.

EXPERT TIP

If you are looking for some other summer vase fillers, add a little beach to any flower arrangement with sea glass, starfish, or sand dollars.

Summer Lights
Dough Bowl

Have you ever seen those day-to-night fashion looks before? The model is wearing the cutest outfit styled with tennis shoes—then in the blink of an eye she changes into heels and adds a scarf and diamond earrings, and suddenly she's ready for date night.

This dough bowl arrangement is a lot like that. It can take the party from day into night.

Start by arranging different greenery stalks in the dough bowl. Here, I mixed faux greenery with greenery bundles from the grocery store. You could also shop your yard for additional greenery.

Then? When your greenery has filled the dough bowl?

Simply add different heights of battery-operated candles to the center of the dough bowl. As the sun sets and night falls, your dough bowl will shimmer and sparkle.

EXPERT TIP
You can add the candles during the day and set them on a timer to light up at night.

Wood Bead
Decorating Ideas

I think we need to start a fan club for strands of wood beads. They are the unsung, underappreciated heroes of the home decor accessory world. They also come in so many colors and styles with tassels and pom-poms. When it comes to decorating with wood beads, the possibilities are endless.

Here are four clever ideas for decorating with wood beads:

- Wrap a wood bead strand around the edge of a cabinet handle. Let the tassels drape down over the cabinet.

- Place wood beads in a bowl on top of a coffee table. Toss them casually over the edge of the bowl to add texture to the display.

- Add wood beads to an outside planter. Wrap them around the rim of the planter and tuck them in among the flowers.

- Place a stack of books at an angle on a table and drape the wood beads and tassels over the edge of the books.

Fruit Pillow DIY

There's something about a pillow that looks good enough to eat. Watermelon is one of my favorite summer fruits, and this easy whimsical DIY pillow looks just like the real thing.

All you need for this simple DIY are two fruit placemats, polyester stuffing, some embroidery thread, and a needle.

Place two watermelon placemats back-to-back and start to stitch the placemats closed. I used a simple running stitch along the edge of the placemats. Continue to stitch until the placemats are stitched together about three-quarters of the way. Fill the opening with polyester pillow stuffing. Don't overfill the pillow with stuffing; simply stuff it enough to add dimension to the stitched placemats.

Then stitch the pillow closed and tie it off at the top with a knot. Your watermelon pillow is ready for summer.

EXPERT TIP
These round placemats come in a variety of fruits.
You could also make pillows with lemons, limes, and grapefruit.

Topiary Kitchen Island Display

Transitioning decor from season to season is almost as challenging as finding the perfect shoes to wear with stirrup pants. Seasons change. Styles change. But one thing remains the same. If you are looking to transition your kitchen island from spring to summer or from summer to fall, you just need one decor item: a topiary.

Topiaries span the seasons. This display is timeless and can take your kitchen island from March to September.

To create this arrangement, start with a low, flat tray or basket. Next, add height to the display with books or pedestals. Finally, add a collection of topiaries to the arrangement. The key to making this topiary kitchen island display work is to use topiaries in different sizes and shapes.

After you place the topiaries on the island, stand back and rearrange to make sure the display looks good from every angle.

EXPERT TIP

Choose topiary pots that are similar in color and sheen to elevate the entire display. For example, use all terra cotta pots or all basket pots or all milk glass.

Watering Can
Front-Door Arrangement

When someone knocks on my front door, I want the door to say hello before I ever get there. This summer door introduces itself in style with a watering can flower arrangement.

To create this look, you'll need a watering can, ribbon, watering picks, flowers, and a door hanger.

Start by trimming the end of the floral stems and attaching a watering pick to each one. This will help the flowers to last longer in the arrangement. Next, add the flowers to the watering can and tie a ribbon around the handle, leaving the ends of the ribbon hanging down. You can use a door hanger or a Command hook to hang the watering can on the door. Tie the arrangement onto the door and fluff the flowers. Your summer door is ready for guests.

EXPERT TIP

If your watering can tilts too much, you can add small stones in the bottom to keep it upright.

How to Decorate
with *Towels*

I remember seeing a bathroom once that had its own towel closet. Rows and rows and rows of towels stacked to the sky. One day my towels might have their very own closet, but for now? I have a simple and easy way to store those towels when space is at a premium.

Add a basket.

I've been adding towels to baskets since my very first home. It's a great way to keep towels fresh, organized, and within easy reach.

Place a low stool or bench near the shower in the bathroom. Add a rectangular basket to the top. Then fold the towels in thirds and add them to a stack in the basket. I also fold hand towels and place them on top. It's so much easier to replace a hand towel in the bathroom when it's neatly folded in a basket.

The next best thing to organizing your towels is decorating with them too.

EXPERT TIP
If folding towels isn't your thing, try rolling them up and placing them inside a taller basket on the floor.

Basket Decorating Ideas

Baskets are my solution to everything. When someone asks me what to put on top of a hutch, I recommend a basket. Looking for a place for throws? A basket works wonders. Need a place for craft supplies? A basket is the perfect solution. When in doubt? Add a basket.

Here are four clever ideas for decorating with baskets:

- Vintage fishing baskets are the perfect place to store craft supplies. Stack them on a stool or line them on the top of a bookcase. The leather latches and classic styling make them beautiful as well as functional.

- Why put silverware away in a drawer when you could place utensils in a basket? They are stored within easy reach, and now the silverware drawer is open for other kitchen items.

- A large basket tucked under a bench is the perfect place to store extra paper towels or disposable kitchen supplies.

- Baskets can also be used to hold greenery and branches.

DIY *Wood Shell* Sign

Have you ever noticed how everything looks better on a signboard? I've added architectural pieces and letters and picture frames and monograms and even coasters. It's such an easy way to create instant artwork with personality.

Like this DIY wood shell sign. Just gather a board, shells, a pencil, craft glue, and a short rope.

To create this project, start with a board—the more distressed the better. Then arrange the shells in the order that you want to put them on the sign. An odd number of shells is best. Use a pencil to mark the dots where you will glue the shells and then use glue to fix the shells in place. Let the glue dry and then add a rope to the back to hang the sign, or you can hang the board directly onto the wall.

EXPERT TIP

If you want to take your sign to the next level, draw a letter on your board with a pencil and then glue shells in place in the shape of the letter.

Hinge *Wreath* Hanger

When I met this hinge, I told it to dream big. And dream it did. This hinge went from hiding in a door jamb to adding an amazing little bit of vintage to this wreath.

It turns out that hinges are actually incredible wreath hangers in disguise.

To recreate this look, start with a vintage hinge. You can find them at thrift stores or yard sales or maybe even your grandmother's junk drawer.

Attach the hinge to a piece of wood (here we've attached it to a window shutter), leaving the center open. Cut approximately 36 inches of ribbon and notch the ends. Thread the ribbon through the center of the hinge and then tie the two ends through a wreath.

Knot and tie a bow to finish the hinge wreath hanger display.

EXPERT TIP

Vintage faucet handles also make amazing wreath hangers. Repeat the steps above with the holes in the faucet handle for a similar look.

How to Update
a *Thrift-Store* Find

Did you know furniture talks to me? We chat at yard sales and thrift stores and even have lengthy discussions on the side of the road. I've discovered so many incredible furniture finds.

Just by listening.

If you are looking for a simple ten-minute update for thrift-store furniture, why not change out the hardware? A quick hardware change is one of the easiest ways to make the piece fit seamlessly with the rest of your decor. Change out dark, outdated hardware with fun brass pulls. It's important to check the existing holes to make sure your hardware will fit. Then unscrew the old hardware, replace it with an updated pull or knob, and start a brand-new conversation.

EXPERT TIP

If you can't find new hardware that you like, consider spray-painting the existing hardware a fun new color for a brand-new look.

Pineapple Vase Grocery-Store Arrangement

I love it when my flower arrangements look like they have been on a cruise. This 10-minute pineapple vase flower arrangement just took a stroll on the Aloha deck. Use a five-dollar grocery-store flower bundle to create this floral display, and your next party will have a centerpiece that's ready for summer.

To create this arrangement, cut off the top of a pineapple. Hollow out the center of the pineapple and set the pineapple pieces aside.

Next, open up the grocery-store bundle and separate the floral stems. Hold them up against the side of the pineapple to judge for height and clip the ends of the stems at an angle. Find a jar or vase that can fit fully inside the pineapple, arrange the flower stems in the vase, and place the vase in the center of the pineapple. Fluff the flowers, and your flower arrangement is ready for a tropical vacation.

EXPERT TIP

Use the pineapple pieces to make an easy summer snack, like fruit skewers with layers of blueberries and strawberries.

DIY *Shell* Napkin Holder

I can still remember the first time I put a conch shell up to my ear and heard the sound of the roaring ocean. Conch shells are one of the prettiest shells on the ocean floor. Large conch shells are often used as sculptures, bookends, or paper weights. But I came up with another idea for the beautiful conch.

A napkin holder. It's the perfect summer accessory.

Next time you are setting your summer table, add a little coastal decor to your party.

Simply take the conch shell and clean it out. Then place a dozen paper napkins vertically in the center of the shell. Mine fit perfectly. It's like the ocean knew the exact dimensions I needed for my square napkins.

EXPERT TIP

You can also use mini conch shells as place-card holders at a party. Tuck a square piece of paper with the name of the guest into the mini conch and add it to their place setting.

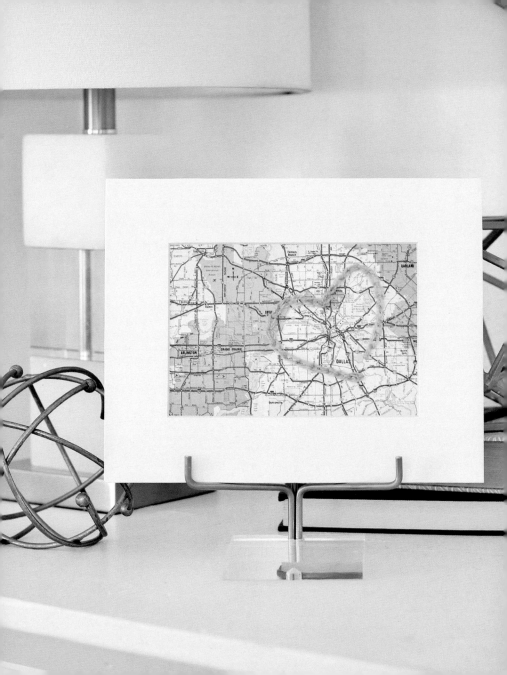

DIY *Map* Art

Someone wise once said that experiences in this world are so much more important than things you can buy. I wish I knew that wise person so I could shake their hand.

Summer is full of experiences. There are trips and vacations and journeys to new destinations. Why not commemorate a summer trip to a special place with this framed DIY map art? All you need is a map of the location you want to celebrate, embroidery thread, a pencil, and an embroidery needle.

With a pencil, lightly draw a heart or a circle around the city or location you are highlighting. Then use the embroidery thread to sew a chain stitch to encircle the spot on the map, following your pencil sketch.

Frame your map and place it on a side table or bookcase to remember the summer journey.

EXPERT TIP

This makes a perfect gift for friends and family who went with you on the journey.

Fall

Don't tell the other seasons, but fall is my favorite. I love sweater weather and clear, crisp afternoons under blue skies with falling leaves to keep the day company. It's like the world is ready for pumpkin spice and hot chocolate.

With all the mini marshmallows.

Here are 18 ideas and projects to get your home ready for fall.

Decorate the Front of a *Hutch*

Sometimes the best ideas are the simplest. I'm kicking off fall with this idea in case you only have five minutes instead of ten. There are so many places to hang a wreath during the fall and winter seasons. And one of the best wreath ideas since sliced bread?

Hang a wreath on the front of a hutch.

But there's a wreath-hanging secret.

If your wreath is a little smaller and doesn't touch the shelf below, sometimes it can lean. If you don't want your wreath to swing on the hutch or tilt backward or forward? Use two suction hooks on the front of the shelf on the hutch instead of one.

Yep. Two hooks are the key instead of one.

This will stabilize the wreath and keep it in place.

EXPERT TIP

Choose a wreath that works with the rest of the fall decor on your hutch, or decorate around it to coordinate.

Transform a
Cutting Board

The other day I almost bought a fancy raised cutting board that would be perfect for a large charcuterie display. It was calling my name with dreams of parties and celebrations and get-togethers. And then? I looked at the price tag.

And I remembered that I have children who need to go to college.

Here's a super simple alternative that is a sixteenth of the price and only takes ten minutes to make.

All you need is a cutting board and four hardware knobs.

Flip the board over and screw in a knob at each corner to raise the board. Make sure your screws for the hardware are not as thick as the cutting board so they don't drill through the top.

Then flip over the board, and it's ready to celebrate.

EXPERT TIP
You can also use the same tip for a tray if you are looking for a footed tray for your next party.

Wood Leaf *Pumpkin*

There are so many ways to make a pumpkin look cute. You can paint them and decoupage them and make your own out of felted wool. The pumpkin-creating possibilities are endless.

If you have pumpkins that have seen better days and need a little refresh, here's a simple tip to make those pumpkins ready for their own fashion show.

Search the aisles of the craft store for wooden leaves. They typically come in a bag with different sizes and shapes. Remove them from the bag and add them to the top of your pumpkins. You can glue them in place, or if the leaves have a small hole at the top like these, you can use a piece of twine to attach them to the pumpkin stem.

EXPERT TIP

Instead of wood leaves, why not add book-page leaves to your pumpkins? Cut out leaves of different shapes and sizes from an old book, pinch the end, and glue them to the top of your pumpkin.

DIY Monogrammed
Doormat

Some people think fall starts in the yard. But around here? Fall starts at the front door. What better way to welcome a new season than with a monogrammed doormat?

To make this personalized doormat you'll need a plain coir or jute doormat, black paint, a stencil, a stencil brush, and painter's tape.

Place the stencil in the center of the doormat. Add painter's tape to hold it in place. Now it's time to create the monogram. Use a stencil brush to make sure your paint doesn't bleed through the edges, and tap the paint on the stencil. Remove the stencil and use painter's tape to create a border around the edges of the mat. Paint inside the tape with black paint and then remove the tape to reveal the border.

Let the doormat dry and then place it outside the front door.

EXPERT TIP
You can also add a three-letter monogram to the doormat instead—or even a personalized fall message.

Fall Pumpkin
Dough Bowl

This pumpkin dough bowl made me laugh out loud. When I added the pumpkins to the center of the dough bowl, they all started arranging themselves.

Truth.

They were all so happy to be together that they just fell into place and snuggled up to each other.

Putting this dough bowl together is just like that. This centerpiece is so easy if you remember one thing: Don't overthink your fall decorating.

Form a layer of wood-slice branches (see page 123) at the bottom of the dough bowl. Next, place four or five larger pumpkins on top of the wood-slice branches. Then add medium pumpkins to the mix, and drop in the smaller pumpkins on top. Let the pumpkins fall where they may. It's usually where they were meant to be and where they are happiest.

I love it when my pumpkins decorate for me.

EXPERT TIP

You can also add leaves to the center of the dough bowl instead of wood slices for a different look.

How to Dry
Eucalyptus

Did you know you can dry eucalyptus?

And in amazing news? Many times it looks even better after it's dried.

I typically purchase eucalyptus in bunches from the grocery store. Then I arrange it on a table or planter and let it dry in place. You can also hang it upside down with jute cording and let it dry in a cool location. Eucalyptus typically takes about a week to completely dry.

Then? It's time to decorate with it.

One of my favorite ways to decorate with dried eucalyptus is to layer it under a pumpkin on a pedestal. Place the pumpkin on the pedestal and then tuck pieces of the eucalyptus underneath. The weight of the pumpkin will hold it in place.

EXPERT TIP

You can also use dried eucalyptus on a mantel or bookshelf. Tuck in pumpkins, gourds, pine cones, and acorns among the leaves for a simple and easy fall project.

Pumpkin Decorating Ideas

I don't think fall decorating is even a thing without pumpkins. Ever since Cinderella showed up at the ball with a pumpkin carriage and mice footmen, pumpkins have been a decorating staple. They are so versatile and work almost everywhere. If you want your home to look like fall? All you have to do is add a pumpkin.

Here are four clever ideas for decorating with pumpkins:

- Pumpkins come in all shapes and sizes. Fill a tiny dough bowl or wood tray with mini pumpkins.

- Velvet pumpkins add texture and an unexpected elegance to pumpkin decorating. Add them to a nest, stack them on books, or simply group them on a side table.

- This fabric pumpkin looks right at home on top of a stack of pillows.

- Layer pumpkins into a collection of white dishes.

Bittersweet Fall Mantel

Just between us? I have a challenging time with fall in my living room. You see, it's blue and white. Not exactly at the top of the fall color list.

And then I came up with a super simple mantel decorating idea, starting with the red orange of bittersweet.

These stems of faux bittersweet look like individual pieces of contemporary art. So I let them shine.

I tucked four long pieces of faux bittersweet on the mantel—two on each side with their stems crisscrossed. Next, I placed blue and white pumpkins among the stems. The key to decorating with pumpkins on a mantel is to vary the height. Use pedestals or books or even milk glass flipped upside down to give height to the pumpkins.

Then I added a few candlesticks and some blue and white pieces.

Now the mantel is ready for fall.

EXPERT TIP

If neutral colors are more your thing, you could recreate the same look with stems of neutral flowers, like dried hydrangea or wheat or dried leaves.

Mini Pumpkin *Garland*

Do you ever get an idea in your head, but then you can't find what you are looking for at the store? When that happens to me, I try to recreate the project on my own.

Like this mini pumpkin garland. I had visions of mini white pumpkins all in a row in a garland.

Good thing it was easy to recreate.

For this project you'll need mini white fabric pumpkins, thread, and a needle. You can usually find pumpkins like these at the craft store in packages of six or eight.

Knot the end of the thread, pull it through the center of the first pumpkin, and continue to thread pumpkins until you have the length of garland you need. After threading the last pumpkin, knot the end of the thread to keep everything in place.

EXPERT TIP

For another fall garland idea, make a pine-cone garland by tying rows of pine cones together with jute twine.

Rustic Fall Place Setting

Planning a fall get-together with family and friends this season? Here's a creative way to set your fall table.

Start with a neutral fall wreath at each place setting, made by wrapping neutral fall stems into a circle with florist wire. Next, place a round cutting board or wood charger on top of the stems. Add a large white plate at each place, layered with a smaller fall leaf plate. Gold silverware, neutral linen napkins (these are my grandmother's), and a beaded napkin ring complete the look.

Finally, scatter pumpkins down the center of the table for an easy centerpiece and add a smaller pumpkin at each place setting as a gift for each of the guests.

EXPERT TIP

For an easy fall centerpiece idea, hollow out faux pumpkins to use as vases in the center of the table.

you've
got
this

Pine-Cone
Decorating Ideas

I miss the pine cones of Kentucky. *Sigh.* They were so plentiful and free. Now that I live in Texas, I buy them in bulk at the craft store. The amazing thing about pine cones? They can take you from fall all the way through February. Just rearrange them a little and adjust for the seasons, and they will be your best decorating friends.

Here are four clever ideas for decorating with pine cones:

- Display your pine cones in rows. Anywhere you have a horizontal surface—windows, shelves, picture ledges and even the base of a chalkboard—you can add a collection of pine cones.

- Mix your pine cones and pumpkins together. Use a large flat tray or container to hold your fall display.

- Add the pine cones to a stack of books. Wrap the books with a velvet ribbon, add a beaded tassel and place a pine cone at the top and bottom of the stack.

- Think outside the box with a pine-cone display in an unusual container, like this vintage truck.

Fall *Flashcard* Display

Every year I open my fall bins to see these fall flashcards staring back at me. And every year I challenge myself to see how I'm going to display them. I ordered them years ago, and they never disappoint. They are so retro and classic and vintage all at the same time.

Over the years, I've added the flashcards to wreaths and centerpieces and chalkboards and taped them onto platters and added them to the plate rack in the kitchen.

But this year I thought I'd try something a little different.

I found these pumpkin place-card holders. They are metal with small metal rings meant for holding a name card.

To create this display, I added a sheaf of wheat, stacks of books, and some pumpkins. Then I tucked the flashcards into the holders and layered them into the display.

EXPERT TIP
You can order flashcards like this off Etsy or simply design your own and print them out on cardstock.

Chair *Swag* DIY

Just when I think I've decorated everything for fall—I've added wreaths to my hutch and garland to my mantel and pumpkins to my table, and I think there's nothing left to add a little fall to—I find another surface.

Chairs. There's nothing cuter than adding a little fall to the back of a chair.

Start with an existing wreath or swag and a little ribbon.

Cut approximately 36 inches of ribbon and notch the ends. Then wrap the ribbon around the chair and tie it in place. If your wreath or swag doesn't have a bow, tie one at the back of the chair. If your swag or wreath is already decorated with a bow, wrap the ribbon around the top of the chair and knot it in place.

Your chairs are ready. Good thing—they like to celebrate fall too.

EXPERT TIP

You can also tie a basket onto the back of a chair and add some fall stems for color and texture.

Pumpkinapalooza
Kitchen Island

Sometimes I wish I could click my heels together and my kitchen island would decorate itself. But my ruby red slippers don't work as well as Dorothy's.

Here are four simple steps you need to create this look for the kitchen island.

1. Start with a flat basket or tray with a lip around the edge to hold the display in place.

2. Add a vintage truck or vintage basket full of pine cones to one side of the basket.

3. Place pumpkins into the center of the basket at varying heights on pedestals or books to stagger the look of the kitchen island display.

4. Tuck neutral branches around the edges of the pumpkins and the truck to finish your fall arrangement.

EXPERT TIP

Dried leaves from the yard also work perfectly in an arrangement like this. Once the leaves turn, collect them from the yard and tuck them in and around the pumpkins.

Fall *Pillow-Cover* DIY

One of the biggest challenges when you switch out your pillows for the season is what to do with the pillows you are replacing.

What if I told you that you don't need to replace the pillows? You can just dress them up.

For this project, start with a table runner that has a matching design on both ends, like the blue and cream runner shown here. You will also need ribbon, a needle, and thread.

Cut the runner to size to cover both sides of your pillow. Next, cut four 8-inch lengths of ribbon.

Fold the trimmed table runner in half and sew a ribbon to each side of the table runner to match on the front and back side. Then slip the table runner over the top of the pillow and tie it in place.

When the season is over, simply remove the runner and store flat until next fall.

EXPERT TIP

You could also sew pillows from each of the ends of the runner. Cut the runner into equal pieces of the desired size, sew three sides, stuff the pillow, and then sew closed.

Wood Bead
Fall Wreath

My grandmother never threw away anything. I still remember the neatly folded sheets of aluminum foil that she kept in her kitchen drawers. I'm not as good at saving things as she was, but one thing I never toss?

A wreath.

It's hard to keep a good wreath down. You can recycle them over and over into new wreaths every year.

Like this wood bead fall wreath.

To make a wreath like this, all you need is a wood bead wreath form, cardboard, some fall foliage, and hot glue.

I cut out a few pieces of cardboard and glued them to the back of the wreath to stabilize the leaves and pumpkins. Then I glued my fall stems to the cardboard, letting them spill over the beads on the front of the wreath.

You can hang the wreath directly on the door or add a bow to the top to hang the wreath from the ribbon.

EXPERT TIP

If you want to recycle a wreath like this later, you can always repaint the beads a new fall color that matches your decor.

Mason Jar Grocery-Store
Flower Arrangement

Did you know that you can dry a flower arrangement in place?

The key is selecting flowers that will dry well with their original color and shape intact. These red pincushion flowers are perfect for an arrangement like this.

For this arrangement, purchase pincushion flowers, eucalyptus, and willow branches from the grocery store. Start by opening the packages and laying out the stems. Remove any stems that are damaged or wilting.

Take three mason jars and fill them three-quarters full with water. Next, trim the stems of the willow branches to be a bit taller than the flowers and greens. Add eucalyptus leaves as a base, then the willow branches, and layer in three stems of pincushion flowers. Trim the flowers to varying lengths for the arrangement.

As the water evaporates from the jar, the flowers and greenery will dry in place.

EXPERT TIP

If your grocery store doesn't carry willow branches, try searching the yard for branches that will work in the arrangement.

Paper-Bag Leaf
Garland

Have you ever seen paper bags look this cute?

This garland is made from recycled paper bags that have been crinkled to look like fall leaves.

To make this DIY you'll need double-stick tape, scissors, and paper bags (you can recycle them from the grocery store—just flip them over so the writing is on the back).

Cut out leaves from the paper bags, about eight inches long. You can use a leaf template or just approximate the leaf shape. Then lightly crinkle them to give the appearance of dried leaves from the yard.

You'll need about 50 paper leaves for a garland like this.

After you cut out the leaves, use double-stick tape to add them to the edge of a bookcase or hutch.

Keep adding leaves until you have the size and shape of garland that you want.

EXPERT TIP

If you don't have paper bags at home, you can always use craft paper to make the leaves instead.

Winter

For me, winter is all about comfort. It's about evergreen branches and Christmas trees and falling snowflakes and candles that smell like pine and sugar cookies that look like they came down a chimney. I like my winter decor like I like my hot chocolate.

Warm and cozy.

Here are 18 ideas and projects to get your home ready for the cozy days of winter.

DIY *Wood-Slice* Branches

I think these DIY wood-slice branches need their own pop album along with pages and pages of iambic pentameter. They take less than 10 minutes to make, and they'll help you decorate your spaces from September to March.

All you need for this easy project are wire branches that look like wood (you can find them online or at local craft stores) and wood slices with pre-drilled holes.

That's it.

Yep. A two-supply craft.

Thread the wire branches through the holes in the wood slices. Twist the ends to attach a wood slice to each branch. Then repeat this step with all the branches until your entire piece is covered.

You can add the branches to a glass vase, place them in a bowl with pine cones, or use them to create a garland on a hutch.

EXPERT TIP

Wire is flexible, so when adding the branches to a display, simply twist and bend them how you want them to look, and the wires will keep them in place.

Bottle-Brush Tree
Window Display

Just typing the words *bottle-brush Christmas trees* makes me happy. They are a little bit of vintage Christmas wrapped up with a wire. The Addis Brush Company first created bottle-brush trees in the 1930s because so many of Britain's real trees had been lost in the war.

And all these years later they are just as popular. They are super inexpensive and come in tons of fun colors and shapes and sizes.

One of the easiest ways to display them is to line them up on a windowsill like this.

Here are a couple of tips to remember for display:

- Line them up about two inches apart on the sill.

- If you don't have enough trees, start on one side and add a few in a row.

- If you mix and match sizes, make sure all sizes are evenly dispersed on the windowsill.

- I like keeping the trees in a similar color family.

EXPERT TIP
If the trees aren't the right color for your decor, you can always spray-paint them to match.

Grocery-Store
Evergreen Arrangement

Creative vases make even the simplest of arrangements so much more fun. I'm always on the lookout for fun, creative containers that look like they could transform into something else.

Like these textured log vases.

I got the faux wood vases years ago, and every winter they show up to help me decorate my Christmas table.

All you need for a winter arrangement like this? Evergreen branches (any kind of branches your grocery store has will work). You can mix cedar, eucalyptus, pine . . . even magnolia or dusty miller will work.

Place the evergreen branches into a smaller vase or mason jar. Insert the smaller container into the log vase. Add the evergreens in the vase. Fluff, and your arrangement is ready to deck the halls.

EXPERT TIP
You can spray-paint the branches and mini pine cones white and add faux snow for more of a wintery arrangement.

Planter Box
Christmas Tree Stand

Did you know that in the first post I ever published on my blog, I forgot a tree skirt? *Truth.*

There was my beautiful Christmas tree covered in neutral and white ornaments with giant plastic feet sticking out in the center of the room.

Just between us? Tree skirts can be a little overrated. There are so many more creative and unique ideas to display your Christmas tree. I've used galvanized buckets and vintage toolboxes and burlap sacks and painted baskets.

But my favorite creative tree stand idea? A planter box.

With so many options and colors and textures, there's a planter box designed to fit any decor.

And the best part? You never have to remember your tree skirt ever again.

EXPERT TIP

You can add casters to the bottom of the planter box to help move the tree around—just be sure to lock them in place when you have the tree where you want it.

Votive *Advent* Calendar

One of the best parts of Christmas is counting down the days until December 25. I love celebrating each and every day of December, and I am the president of any Advent calendar's fan club.

Here's a creative display idea to help mark off the days on your calendar.

I purchased 25 votive candle holders with the numbers 1 through 25 on the front. If you can't find a set like this, you can always DIY your own with vinyl cutouts.

Instead of filling them with candles, I added one ornament to the top of each votive. I used additional ornaments to decorate the Advent display.

The only thing that's more fun than an Advent calendar is one you can decorate with too.

EXPERT TIP

You could also insert a Scripture verse into each votive to pull out and read on the day you add the ornament to the votive.

Christmas Ornament
Dough Bowl

If you stopped by my house right about October, you'd see 37 Christmas totes making their way down from the attic. Each one is full to the brim of Christmas. There are Christmas trees and Christmas sleighs and Christmas jingle bells. And when I empty them, there's always something left over at the bottom of the tote: Christmas ornaments.

There are large ornaments and small ornaments and medium ornaments all needing a home.

No worries. I came up with a solution for all those stray Christmas ornaments. I added them to a dough bowl.

To create a display like this, just fill your dough bowl to the brim with ornaments of all shapes, sizes, and textures. Add a few pine cones or other decorations, fluff and arrange, and you have a creative centerpiece for Christmas.

EXPERT TIP
I kept all my ornaments in the same color family, but you could add multicolored ornaments or even gold and silver for a similar display.

Ornament *Wreath* Display

If there was a Christmas wreath contest, this wreath would easily win Miss Congeniality. Just look at that sparkling personality!

And it's so easy to make an ornament wreath like this happier and brighter and merrier with one simple ten-minute decorating tip—hang the wreath on a mirror.

The reflection of the shiny ornaments in the mirror instantly doubles the impact and the decorating possibilities.

To hang a wreath like this on a mirror, you'll just need a sturdy Command hook. Attach the Command hook to the upper part of the center of the mirror, press it in place, and then hang the wreath. Make sure the mirror is larger than the wreath so the wreath is reflected in the glass.

EXPERT TIP

You can find wreaths like this online and in stores, or you could DIY your own using a metal wreath form, hot glue, ornaments of various colors and sizes, and a little tinsel garland or other flexible material to fill in the gaps.

Tree-Covered Kitchen Island

I'm always trying to think of ways to make my winter decorating last way past Christmas. Then after Christmas leaves the building, the winter decor will last until spring.

Like this kitchen island. It's full of trees. At Christmas time they are Christmas trees . . . and then?

In January, they transform themselves into winter trees. This is the perfect display for all those cold and chilly winter months.

To create a display like this, start collecting Christmas trees. You can find them at yard sales and thrift stores in all sizes and shapes. Look for trees with different textures and varied leaves.

Get a large basket or tray to contain the display, and you may want to add height with pedestals or books or containers flipped upside down. Then place in the trees.

Check the arrangement from all sides. This is super important on something like a kitchen island in the center of a room.

EXPERT TIP
If you don't have enough mini trees to fill out the display, you can always use branches to add more winter to the display.

Creative *Linen* Storage Idea for the Holidays

Have you ever found something that you loved but had no idea how to use?

And in amazing news? You bought it anyway.

Oh, good. Me too.

Meet my "no idea what to do with but bought it anyway" vintage metal storage container. I found this at a yard sale and had to have it. Sometime long ago it was probably used to store hardware or tools. Instead? I use it for a creative storage idea.

I brought it home and cleaned it off and decided it was the perfect place to store extra linens and cutlery I need at the last minute for holiday celebrations. I layered my collection of extra cutlery and linens into each of the drawers of the metal piece. The size and depth of the drawers are perfect for storing my entire collection.

EXPERT TIP

Depending on the age and color of your linens, you may want to line the drawers to prevent any damage to the linens.

Sleigh Centerpiece

You are looking at one of the best yard-sale decisions I ever made. This sled was sad and a little forlorn and sitting on top of a plastic table along with some bingo cards and a couple of electric guitars that were missing a few strings.

I took it home and spray-painted it white. And every year at Christmas, I pull it out and fill it with ornaments for an easy centerpiece idea.

Decorating with ornaments is one of my favorite low-cost, time-saving holiday decorating tips. Scatter them with greenery on your dining table, tie them on top of a present, add them to a wreath, or—like here—use them to fill a yard-sale sleigh to the brim.

The moral of this sleigh tale? Never walk away from a sleigh keeping company with musical instruments.

EXPERT TIP

If you don't have a sleigh like this, look around your house for an everyday container like an oversized platter and fill it with ornaments instead.

Pom-Pom Christmas Tree Pillow

Sometimes I want my Christmas trees to be bright and merry. And then sometimes I just want a little neutral for my Christmas decor.

This pom-pom pillow adds a little neutral holiday cheer to a bench or chair.

To make this pillow, you'll need a burlap pillow cover, approximately 28 white pom-poms (depending on size), a wood cork, fabric glue, cardboard, and a cup of coffee.

Dye the pom-poms in coffee to give them a vintage feel. Simply brew the coffee (or you can use tea for a lighter pom-pom) and submerge the pom-poms for 30 minutes. Allow them to dry overnight.

Place a piece of cardboard inside the pillow cover, then arrange the pom-poms in a triangle on the center of the front of the pillow cover. Glue them in place with fabric glue. For the tree stem, glue half of a wood cork or a wooden spool to the pillow at the base of the tree.

Remove the cardboard and add the pillow insert to the finished pillow cover after everything dries. Your pillow is ready to celebrate.

EXPERT TIP

You can also trim your pillow with a neutral velvet ribbon to add additional embellishments to the design.

Pine-Cone
Front-Door Hanger

Hello, holiday front door. Nice to meet you.

This is the perfect front-door display to take you from Christmas into the winter months that follow.

To make this front-door hanger, you'll need a large jump ring, small eye hooks, ribbon, fabric glue, and flocked pine cones.

Start by screwing the eye hooks into the end of each pine cone. Thread the ribbon through the eye hook and the large jump ring and glue the ends together to create a big loop. Repeat these steps for each of the pine cones until you have the number of hanging pine cones you need for your display. Vary the length and size of the ribbon loops so the pine cones hang at different lengths.

Then tie the pine-cone hanger to the door using a Command hook, wreath hanger, or even the door knocker.

EXPERT TIP

You can also spray-paint the pine cones or add glitter or even gold foil to create a completely different look with your display.

Creative *Nativity* Displays

Someone wise once said, "Jesus is the reason for the season." My nativity sets and I couldn't agree more.

There's something so special about a nativity set with Mary and Joseph and the shepherds and the wise men and baby Jesus. Each year when I pull out the nativity sets (some of which have been handed down from my grandmother), I'm reminded why we celebrate Christmas.

Here are some creative and unique ideas to display nativity sets:

- My grandmother hand-stitched this nativity set for me. I love displaying it under the tree on a wooden box or vintage container at the base of the Christmas tree.

- Place it on a pedestal. My mother made a beautiful nativity set for me, and I display it every year on a cake stand.

- Add an Advent calendar to your nativity set. Surround the nativity with the countdown to Jesus's birth.

- Add a nativity set to a wreath. Use glue or wire to attach a plastic or fabric nativity set to the center of a wreath.

EXPERT TIP

In our family tradition, Jesus doesn't appear in the nativity until December 25. On Christmas morning, we place him in the manger.

DIY Pine-Cone
Snowflake

I didn't really grow up with snowflakes. I lived in Texas, where snow-flakes are as rare as unsweetened tea. Maybe that's why they've always fascinated me. Since I didn't have snowflakes, I had to make my own.

Like this DIY pine-cone snowflake.

To create your very own snowflake made of pine cones, you'll need a wood board, mini pine cones, hot glue, and a pencil.

Sketch the outline of a snowflake on the wood board. For mine, I drew one horizontal line, one vertical line and then two diagonal lines.

Glue the first mini pine cone in the center of the penciled-in snow-flake. Then continue to glue pine cones along the penciled lines until the lines are covered.

At the tips of each diagonal line, glue two smaller lines of pine cones to create the look of a snowflake.

Remove any excess glue, and your snowflake is ready for winter.

EXPERT TIP
If you don't have a piece of wood, this project is perfect for an old canvas or even an old tray.

Vintage Holiday
Place Setting

When you're setting a table for family and friends for the holidays, all you really need to do is shop the Christmas boxes in your attic.

You'll see. Those boxes are full of Christmas decorations just waiting for you to ask them to dinner.

Here are a few fun ideas for setting the table for the holidays:

- Use a patterned mini stocking to hold silverware. Tuck a stocking at each guest's place and add their napkin and silverware inside.

- Layer a special ornament on each place setting with a sprig of evergreen. Then guests can take the ornament home as a party gift.

- For inexpensive table decor, decorate the table centerpieces with greenery and ornaments and small presents wrapped with ribbon.

- Instead of a charger, use a wreath or greenery under each of the place settings and anchor the place setting with a cutting board.

- Small vintage milk bottles are also perfect for serving cookies and milk for dessert.

Mini Tree
Decorating Ideas

Can I tell you the best decorating tip Santa ever gave me? *Shhhh.* Don't let the elves know, but I decorate with my trees. I've been collecting them for years (especially the small ones) and adding them around the house for some extra evergreen cheer.

Here are four clever ideas for decorating with trees:

- Display your trees in collections. For example, I display an entire branch tree collection on top of a tool box in the family room.

- DIY your own wood trees. My brother made these wood trees from pallet wood. He cut one tree out of a row of wood pieces and framed the other tree with pallet wood. I use them to decorate a mantel with battery operated candles and garland.

- Add mini banners to your trees. Print out banners on the computer in a holiday font, cut them in strips, notch the ends, and glue them to the front of a mini tree.

- Place snow-covered trees in a grouping of three and stack them on a set of books to vary the height.

Wood *Noel* Blocks

Raise your hand if you like a little trash-to-treasure project. Oh, good—me too. There's something about trash that wants to live a better life that touches my heart. These wood blocks are actually pieces of molding I was going to throw away. We worked on a DIY project at the house, and these were left over. I picked them up to toss, and the blocks raised their eyebrows at me.

And an idea popped into my head.

All you need for this project are leftover pieces of molding (or any kind of wood blocks), paint, chipboard letters, and wood glue. You can usually find chipboard letters in the scrapbooking section of the craft store.

Paint the molding and the chipboard letters. I used gray and white craft paint. Once the paint is dry, lightly sand the edges of the blocks to distress them. Last, glue a chipboard letter to the front of each wood block. I used four blocks and glued the letters *N-O-E-L*.

EXPERT TIP

This project actually works throughout all four seasons just by choosing a word that's designed for that season.

Wood-Slice
Christmas Tree

I've made a lot of DIY Christmas trees. There was the Scrabble-letter Christmas tree and the twig Christmas tree and the paper Christmas tree. I even have a fabric Christmas tree someone made for me out of my bridesmaids' dress material.

But this wood-slice Christmas tree? I think it's one of the easiest trees I've ever made.

All you need for this project is a framed piece of wood or decorative tray, wood slices, and hot glue. The tree is actually a puzzle. I bought a package of wood slices of various sizes from the craft store and arranged them in a triangle. It takes a little creative maneuvering to make the wood slices work into the right shape. Just keep moving them around until you have a Christmas tree.

Once you have them arranged, glue the slices to the base. Then add a slice at the bottom and a paper star at the top to finish off the Christmas tree.

EXPERT TIP
You could also add a metal or wood star to the top of the tree to add another texture to the wood-slice Christmas tree.

Conclusion

Can I tell you how much joy I have right now?

I can't help it. It was an amazing year. I got to decorate through all the seasons with you.

And now that we are friends? This is my hope for you: I hope you leave these pages inspired. I hope you design and plan and decorate your spaces to be truly yours. I hope you create a home that YOU love.

But most importantly? I hope you understand that decorating does NOT have to be complicated or overwhelming or intricate or elaborate or complex.

Truth? Decorating is all about making one tiny change after another—taking the entire decorating process one step at a time. Then when you stand back and look? You'll see how all those small changes fit together to turn a house into a home.

And now?

Want to start the year again?

Oh good. I've got 10 more minutes.

How about you?

About the Author

KariAnne Wood writes the award-winning lifestyle blog *Thistlewood Farms*, a tiny corner of the internet where all the stories and DIYs hang out and drink sweet tea. She also writes, photographs, and styles for several national magazines, including *Better Homes and Gardens*, *Romantic Homes*, *Country Women*, and *Flea Market Décor*. KariAnne is the author of *The DIY Style Finder*, *But Where Do I Put the Couch?*, and *52 DIY Crafts for Girls*. This fun-loving rockstar mother of four lives in Dallas with her husband.

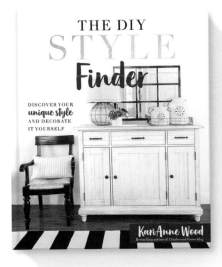

THE DIY
STYLE
Finder

DISCOVER YOUR
unique style
AND DECORATE
IT YOURSELF

KariAnne Wood
Bestselling author of *Thistlewood Farms* blog

BUT WHERE
DO I PUT
the couch?

&

Answers to 100 Other
Home Decorating Questions

Melissa Michaels
The Inspired Room

KariAnne Wood
Thistlewood Farms

Published in association with William K. Jensen Literary Agency,
119 Bampton Court, Eugene, Oregon 97404.

Cover and interior design by Nicole Dougherty

Photos on pages 128, 130, 132, 134, 136, 140, 146, 152 by Kenna Lynn Photo.
All other photography by KariAnne Wood.

For bulk or special sales, please call 1-800-547-8979.
Email: Customerservice@hhpbooks.com

TEN PEAKS PRESS is a trademark of the Hawkins Children's LLC.
Harvest House Publishers, Inc., is the exclusive licensee of this trademark.

10-Minute Decorating Ideas
Text and photographs copyright © 2023 by KariAnne Wood
Published by Ten Peaks Press, an imprint of Harvest House Publishers
Eugene, Oregon 97408

ISBN 978-0-7369-8763-9 (hardcover)
ISBN 978-0-7369-8764-6 (eBook)

Library of Congress Control Number: 2023930377

Printed in China

23 24 25 26 27 28 29 30 31 / RDS—ND / 10 9 8 7 6 5 4 3 2 1